SURFING

Paul Mason

WAYLAND

to the limit
SURFING

Other titles in this series

BLADING

MOTOCROSS

MOUNTAIN BIKING

SKATEBOARDING

SNOWBOARDING

First published in 2000 by Wayland
Copyright © Wayland 2000
Revised and updated 2008

Wayland   Wayland Australia
338 Euston Road   Level 17/207 Kent Street
London NW1 3BH   Sydney NSW 2000

Produced for Wayland by Roger Coote Publishing,
Gissing's Farm, Fressingfield, Eye, Suffolk IP21 5SH
Project Management: Mason Editorial Services
Designer: Tim Mayer

A catalogue record for this book is available from the British Library.

ISBN 978 0 7502 5419 9

Printed in China

Wayland is a division of Hachette Children's Books,
an Hachette Livre UK company.
www.hachettelivre.co.uk
Note:
In preparation of this book, all due care has been taken
with regard to the advice, activities and exercises depicted.
The Publishers cannot accept liability for any injury or loss
sustained. When learning a new sport, it is important to seek
expert tuition and to follow a manufacturer's advice.

WARNING!
Surfing is a dangerous sport. This book is full
of advice, but reading it won't keep you safe
in the ocean. Take responsibility for your own
safety, and get lessons.

WHAT IS

Surfing is the art of riding waves. There are lots of different ways of doing this: on a kneeboard, a bodyboard, using just your body and a set of swim fins, or on an inflatable mat. But most people surf on… a surfboard!

SURFING?

Surfing looks simple, but is actually incredibly hard to learn. Once you've learnt, though, you never forget how. There are fifty, sixty and seventy-year-old people surfing today, who learnt back when surfing first became popular. On the same beaches as these older surfers are kids of five or six years old, just catching their first waves: the first of thousands, or tens of thousands, of waves they'll ride in their lifetime.

Startup Vocabulary Kit

Session	The time from when you paddle out until you ride your last wave into the beach.
"Out there"	Out catching waves; also, not here, on the land.
Gnarly	Difficult, aggressive or, especially, dangerous.
Dude	Another surfer. Be careful with this word: one month it's cool to use it, the next it's not.
Betty	Girl. A surf betty is, of course, a surfer girl.
Out the back	Out beyond the spot where the waves break.
Lineup	Where the waves break, where surfers wait to catch them.
Rights	A wave on which you turn to the right.
Lefts	A wave on which you turn left.

He'enalu

The Hawaiian word for surfing is *he'enalu*. It comes from two separate words; like many Hawaiian words each has several meanings:

He'e (v.)

1 To ride a surfboard. 2 To flee; to flee through fear.

Nalu (v.)

1 To speak secretly, or to speak to one's self. 2 To think; to search after any truth or fact.

So, surfing is to ride a surfboard; also, perhaps, to flee in fear, and to search for the truth.

Roots

Surfing was born in Hawaii, where riding the best boards, called *olos*, was allowed only by kings. It first spread to the rest of the world in 1907, when George Freeth came from Hawaii to demonstrate surfing at Redondo Beach in California. But the first famous surfer was Duke Kahanamoku. Duke spread surfing to mainland USA, and to Australia on a visit there in 1914.

Five Great Surfing Films

- *The Endless Summer*
- *Big Wednesday*
- *Five Summer Stories*
- *Morning of the Earth*
- *Thicker than Water*

The view from the lifeguard tower at Pipeline, Hawaii. Surfers looked at this break for years before anyone dared to paddle out.

Surfing Spreads to Europe

Surfing was brought to Europe by the film industry, but not because people saw surfing at the cinema and wanted to have a go. Instead, two movie-makers working on a film of Ernest Hemingway's novel *The Sun Also Rises* saw the excellent waves of the western French coast near Biarritz. They got hold of some boards and went out to surf: a new sport had arrived in Europe!

Surfers desparate to get to the beach have even sometimes stolen bikes from small children.

Surfing has been around for many years, but first became widely popular in the 1960s. The message was spread by the surf movie. The first movies were made by surfers themselves, but Hollywood soon caught on. Tens of thousands of kids were introduced to surfing by movies such as *Muscle Beach Party* and *Gidget*.

Duke Kahanamoku

Duke was not only a great surfer, but he was also the best swimmer in the world, and won gold medals at the 1912 and 1920 Olympics. He was only finally beaten by Johnny Weismuller, who went on to star as Tarzan in several movies.

Duke himself was also a film star, and played a variety of roles in Hollywood movies. He even acted with another 'Duke', John 'Duke' Wayne, in *The Wake Of the Red Witch*.

Shortboards

Many surfers today ride shortboards. These are slimline performance boards that allow the most radical manoeuvres because of their light weight and speed. They're also much harder to ride than longboards (Malibus) or mini-mals.

Although they look very similar, even slight changes to a shortboard's shape can make it ride very differently. The key elements are length, width, thickness and bottom shape.

Surfboard Design Variables:

Thick rail

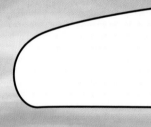

Thin rail

Rail shape

A thick, round rail is easier to control but slower to turn; a hard, thin rail is quicker-turning, but catches in the water if the surfer isn't skilful.

Tail shape

Narrower tails cling to steep waves; wider tails accelerate better but are harder to control.

--- Nose

A wider nose catches waves better; a narrower nose is easier to ride in steep waves.

--- Length

Longer, wider boards catch waves better; shorter, narrower ones are easier to turn.

--- Bottom shape

Concaves or channels around the fins drive water under the board, making it faster. Vee makes a board more manoeuvrable, but needing more 'push' from the wave.

Vee

Single concave

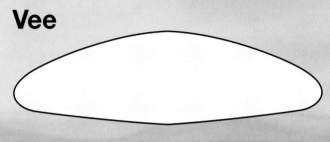

Favourite Dimensions

The legendary Californian shaper and Channel Islands founder Al Merrick suggests the following:

Type:	Dimensions:	Bottom shape:
Small wave board	6'0"-6'6"x19"x $2^3/_8$"	Single to double concave
Larger-wave board	6'8"-7'0"x18.5"x $2^1/_4$"	Variable vee throughout

-- Fins

Fins of different sizes make a board go quicker or slower, and affect manoeuvrability.

The Retro
Movement

Dave Rastovich, famous for his love of twin-fins, ripping on one at Cape Verde.

Twinnie Revolution

The twin-fin or 'twinnie' is probably the most popular new surfboard of the last few years. Twinnies have short, wide tails and two big fins. They combine the fast-turning of a shortboard with the wave-catching of a longboard.

For the last few years 'retro' boards have become more and more popular. The first retro boards were longboards, copies of 9' long boards from the 1960s. Inspired by the 'longboard revolution', shapers began making other boards that were influenced by the past.

Getting five toes over the nose of the board like this is called 'hanging five'.

Good Things About Longboards

- Catch loads of waves
- Paddle well
- Stable and easy to learn on

And Some Bad Things

- Often ridden (dangerously) by beginners
- Greedy riders seem never to give waves away

Joel Tudor

Joel Tudor was 17 when he first won the World Longboard Championship. He now spends most of his time travelling around the world, making appearances for his sponsor and surfing in competitions or for photo shoots.

Who says surfing's hard? Not Joel.

The retro movement has made it cool to ride all kinds of surfboard. Ten years ago, lots of people thought 'proper' surfers rode only shortboards. These days a mixture of retro boards can be spotted in most lineups. Now, surfers who can afford more than one board might have a shortboard, a twin-fin or 'twinnie', a longboard, and a single-fin in their shed – each waiting for just the right day to be ridden.

Duane Desoto tuberiding on a longboard.

BASICS AND STYLE

Every surfer in the world has his or her own style. Some are super-cool, hardly seeming to move. Others look like a whirlwind, with arms and legs twisting and turning all over the place.

Whatever your style, it's made up of five basic moves. All the rest are just window dressing.

1 The Takeoff

Paddle hard to get the board moving. As it starts to catch the wave, push down on the deck and whip your feet through. Sounds easy. It isn't.

2 The Bottom Turn

You're on your feet, flying down the face of the wave. To go along the wave, instead of in front of it, you need to turn to the side, ahead of the white water. Crouching, lean hard into the rail of the board. Take your weight off the rail only as the board comes round.

The Top Turn

3

Timing is everything! To avoid flying off the back of the wave, you need to turn back down its face. It's a bottom turn in reverse. Kind of.

The Floater

A section of the wave crumbles in front of you: turn around the bottom, or float over the top. To pull a floater, hit the top of the wave and keep your board pointing along it. To do this, it has to *feel* as though you're making your board point out of the back of the wave.

The Cutback

Once in a while, you get too far ahead of the steep, fast bit of the wave. A hard turn back the way you came (and then another one to point you the right way again) is called a cutback.

More style still

Almost all surfing moves are based on the bottom turn, top turn, floater or cutback, but surfers have found more and more variations on these themes. Many surfers also ride skateboards and some go snowboarding: skateboarding, especially, has fed some radical moves into surfing. At beaches around the world you can see kids floating aerials, doing tailslides, reverses, 360s and a load of other seemingly impossible tricks.

The Air Show

When aerials first appeared in surfing, there was no real attempt to land them and carry on surfing. Today, though, most young contest surfers include aerials in their bag of tricks, and there are even special contests called 'air shows'.

One of the original aerialists, Shane Beschen, pushing the boundaries of what's possible on a surfboard.

Definitely Not Stylish

- Day-glo wetsuits
- Tight, short surf trunks
- Permed hair
- Aggro
- Dropping in (see page 24)

Competition

The Eddie

The Quiksilver In Memory Of Eddie Aikau, or 'The Eddie' as surfers call it, is a special competition. You must be invited to enter, and the competition is held only if the waves at Waimea Bay, Hawaii are more than twenty feet high. The competition is held to remember Eddie Aikau, a famous Hawaiian lifeguard and surfer, who died tragically at sea.

Most surfers never enter a competition, and there's no rule that says you should. But the best surfers end up competing, because it's almost the only way to make a living as a surfer.

The top surfing competition is the ASP (Association of Surfing Professionals) World Championship Tour. This is made up of the Top 44 surfers in the world, plus others who qualify to compete against them in each event. Feeding into the ASP are qualifying competitions that take place all around the world. These are grouped under the umbrella name WQS, or World Qualifying Series.

As well as these competitions there are one-offs like the Eddie Aikau memorial contest, and national and regional contests.

The lefthander at G-land is home to one of the world's biggest – and most remote – surfing contests.

The World Tour

MONTH	LOCATION	COUNTRY
February/March	Kirra/Gold Coast	Australia
	Bell's Beach	Australia
May	Teahupoo	Tahiti
May/June	Tavarua/Namotu	Fiji
July	Jeffrey's Bay	South Africa
July/August	Western Australia	Australia
September	Southwest France	France
	Trestles	USA
September/October	Mundaka	Spain
October/November	Catarina	Brazil
December	Pipeline, Oahu	Hawaii

A surfer competing at
Pipeline, Hawaii, claims
big points from the judges.

The World's Greatest Surfer

One afternoon in December, 1995, one surfer won the Chiemsee Pipe Masters, the Hawaiian Triple Crown of Surfing, and his third World Championship. Kelly Slater has since won more world championships, taking his total in 2008 to eight. He is, unquestionably, the greatest surfer in the world.

The heat where the 1995 world title was won: Slater cheers on his friend Rob Machado.

Slater Fact File

Kelly Slater was born and brought up in Florida, on the East Coast of the USA. He lived 20 minute's drive from Sebastian Inlet, the East Coast's most famous surf spot, and surfed there every day there were waves.

As well as being the most successful surfer ever, Slater has dated a string of beautiful women, including Pamela Anderson and Giselle Bundchen. And (just in case you didn't think he was perfect yet) he also supports several charities.

Beach celebrations for another world championship.

Slater on his Third World Title

"Last year's Pipe was definitely the best contest I've had in my life. I'm sure it'll always be that for me. I really don't think anything could ever top that."

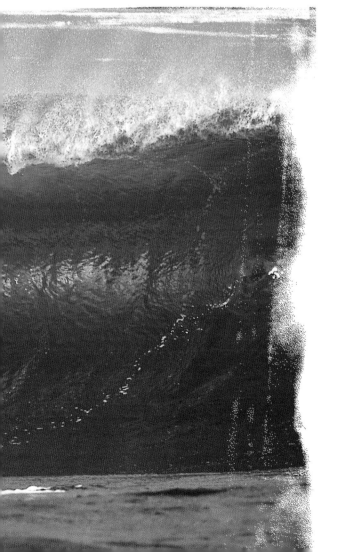

Surf photographers brave the impact zone in the effort to get a picture of the world's most successful surfer.

HAWAII

Hawaii is at the heart of surfing. It's where the world championship is often decided. Every surfer dreams of going to the North Shore for the winter season. This is when some of the biggest waves in the world are ridden.

Welcome to Hawaii...

Localism

Hawaii is the world's most overcrowded surfing location, and localism is common there. Localism is when surfers from a particular spot try to discourage other people from coming there. At its mildest, it just means local surfers aren't very friendly to visitors. At its strongest, it can lead to violence and destruction of surfboards and other property.

Haoles

Hawaiians call non-Hawaiian surfers *haoles*. The word was first used when Europeans arrived in the islands with Captain Cook. It meant 'without the breath of life, foreigner, or white man.' Later, the invasion of Hawaii by Europeans following Cook was mirrored by an invasion of Hawaiian beaches by surfers from elsewhere, and the word began to be used again to describe the newcomers.

... land of the super-grommet...

Hawaii is where surfing comes from. Duke Kahanamoku spread surfing out from Hawaii in the 1910s and 1920s, and in the 1950s Hawaii was where the best American surfers came to test themselves. It's still the ultimate proving ground.

... and the telephoto lens. Well, would you take water shots in those waves?

Big Waves

For some surfers, the ultimate challenge is to surf in big waves. Surfing is always dangerous, but big-wave surfers risk their lives with every session. In recent years, two of the best surfers in the world, Mark Foo and Todd Chesser, have been killed in big surf.

Big-wave surfers ride larger boards (about 9' long) which help them catch the waves.

Mavericks

One of the most famous big-wave spots is Mavericks' Reef in Half Moon Bay, California. Cold water and currents add to a steep takeoff and dangerous rocks to make this one of the most challenging waves anywhere. It's also part of the Red Triangle – where there are regular attacks on surfers by great white sharks.

Tow-in Boards

The ingredients of a tow-in board are as follows:

Heavy, thick glass coat
For strength and to weight the board down.

Lead core
To weight the board down and stop it bouncing off the face of the wave.

Shorter length
Easier to turn. No need for easy paddling.

Footstraps
Keep the surfer's feet attached to the board as it's being towed and while riding huge waves.

Big-wave riders continue to push the boundaries. Tow-in surfing is now popular around the world. Surfers riding specialist boards are towed along by jet skis, to match the speed of giant open-ocean waves (impossible if you're paddling in the normal way). They release the tow line just as the wave is about to break, and ride the wave using natural power.

Laird Hamilton tow-in surfing at Peahi, also known as 'Jaws'. Laird is 6′ tall, so how big is this wave face?

The Largest Wave

Greg Noll, otherwise known as Da Bull, paddled out into giant surf on the North Shore of Oahu, Hawaii and rode down the face of a wave that spectators agreed was at least 40 feet high. He then fell off. No one on the beach thought he could possibly survive, but Da Bull's head appeared in the white water and he swam to shore.

Ethics

Surfers can seem like rebels – it's an image some of them love. But there are rules about how to behave while you're surfing, which are sometimes strictly enforced.

If you think about it, it makes sense to have a set of rules that everyone agrees to. Surfing's dangerous enough as it is: if there was anarchy in the lineup, injuries and accidents would be common.

Crowds in the lineup can equal injuries, so surfers have their own rules about how to behave safely.

Surfing's rules are there to help everyone, and most people are happy to go along with them. But be warned: stories of offenders having the fins punched off their boards, their car windscreen plastered in surf wax, or even worse, are common.

See how the surfers below are checking left and right to see who should ride the wave.

Priority Quiz

1 Five people are all paddling for the same wave. Who gets to ride it?

a) the surfer with the coolest board;

b) the oldest surfer;

c) the surfer taking off closest to the peak, where the wave first breaks.

2 You're riding in on the best wave you've caught all day. Someone paddling out is right in your path. What do you do?

a) start hurling abuse at them and waving them out of the way;

b) try to turn round them;

c) straighten out or turn off the wave, so you're sure you won't hurt them.

3 You're paddling out and a wave breaks in front of you. There are probably other people paddling out behind. What's the best thing to do?

a) dump your board and dive as deep as you can. It probably won't hit anyone;

b) check behind you before letting it go;

c) hang on to your board and duck dive or roll it. Even if there's no one behind you, it's good practice.

How Did You Do?

Mostly a) – you are a complete lame-brain. You shouldn't be allowed outside, let alone out surfing. If you do go out surfing, it won't be long before you're sent back to the beach.

Mostly b) – there is hope: you're not deliberately dangerous, and respect for your elders is a good thing.

Mostly c) – you will be welcome on most beaches, because you're not going to hurt anyone.

Ocean Safety

Imagine someone throwing a bucketful of water at your face, and think how the force of it would push your head back. How many buckets of water do you think there are in even a small wave, and how much damage could they do to your body?

SURFING IS DANGEROUS. Currents, big waves, shallow bottoms, other surfers, rocks – all can catch you out unless you take care. And we haven't even mentioned sharks…

Above: Snapped boards like this show how powerful waves can be. Below: The worst wipeout ever? Nope.

Safety Tips

- Never surf alone.

- Never surf when there are warning flags out.

- When you fall off, tuck your chin in and, with your forearm in front of your face, wrap one hand over your head. Wrap the other arm round the back of your neck. This keeps your neck from being snapped back and stops your board hitting you in the head.

- Always jump off away from your board, so there's less chance of it hitting you.

- Unless there are rocks in front, it's safest to straighten out in front of the wave and lie down on your board, rather than jumping backwards into the white water.

Currents

If you find yourself caught in a current:

● Don't panic.

● Don't try to paddle against the current. You can never be stronger than the ocean.

● Stay with your board.

● Paddle sideways out of the current. It will continue to sweep you along, but you'll be heading towards the edge, where there will be slower water.

● Once in slower water, head for land.

It's hard to work out if this is worse for the surfer bailing out or the bodyboarder paddling.

Famous Spots

Pretty much anywhere that waves break you can find people trying to ride them. Some spots have been ridden for years; others have only just been discovered; still others are rarely ridden because they're so hard to get to.

Every surfing region has its famous spots. Some kinds of wave are more common in particular places, but generally any area will have a scattering of each kind of wave: reef breaks, beach breaks and point breaks.

Canary Islands.

West Coast California, USA.

Hawaiian reef break.

Point Breaks

Point breaks make waves that roll along a point of land that sticks out to sea. They break evenly, although sometimes quite slowly, and give excellent long rides.

Two famous examples: Jeffrey's Bay, South Africa; Malibu, USA

Jeffrey's Bay, South Africa.

Seignosse, western France.

Reef Breaks

So called because the waves break over reefs, either close to shore or far out to sea. These waves usually break fast and hard, in shallow water and in a fairly predictable way.

Two famous examples: Pipeline, Hawaii; Uluwatu, Bali.

Balinese reef break, Indonesia.

Bells Beach, Australia.

Beach Breaks

Of course, these break off the beach, on a bottom of either sand or mixed sand and rock. Although not usually as fierce as reef breaks, beach breaks are unpredictable and often hard to surf well.

Two famous examples: Supertubes, Portugal; Johanna, Australia.

The Box, Western Australia.

Glossary

Word:	Means:	Doesn't mean:
Dropping in	Taking off in front of another surfer who has right of way.	Popping by to visit your friends.
Grommet	Young surfer.	Anything to do with DIY.
Ho-dad	Non-surfer; an uncool person.	'Hello, Father!'
Kahuna	Hawaiian royalty; older (much older), respected surfer.	Anything to do with beefburgers.
Localism	Aggression from local surfers aimed at keeping others away.	Pride in your community.
Olo	Super-long, super-heavy hardwood board used by old-time *kahunas*.	Hello in Norwegian.
Peak	Place in which the wave first breaks.	Mountain.
Rail	Thin edge of a surfboard.	Thing trains run on.
Rocker	The amount of curve a board has, viewed from the side.	Person dressed in a leather jacket who likes Aerosmith.
Stringer	Thin strip of wood in the middle of a board for strength.	Piece of string.
Taking off	Starting to ride a wave.	Disappearing; running away.
Malibu	Another name for a longboard; also, the Southern California beach where they first became popular.	A horrid alcoholic drink.
Wahine	Girl or woman.	Exclamation during wipeout.

Books

Fiction:

The Dogs Of Winter Kem Nunn (No Exit Press, 1998), and *Tapping The Source* Kem Nunn (No Exit Press, 1997): two adult but beautifully written novels set in California.

Non- fiction:

Walking On Water Andy Martin (Minerva Press): the musings of a Cambridge professor and surfing enthusiast who finds himself on the North Shore of Hawaii one winter season.

Diary of a Surf Freak Dan Johnson (Heinemann Library, 2003)

Magazines

There are more surfing magazines than we've got room for here, but a few of the best are *Carve* magazine (U.K. based); *Surfer* and *Surfing* (monthly American magazines); and *Tracks* and *ASL* (both monthly Australian surfing magazines).

Websites

The magazines listed above all have good websites, listing competition results, biographies of top surfers, surfing history and sometimes even a surfcheck.

The Association of Surfing Professionals also has a good website for keeping up with competition news, at *www.aspworldtour.com*.

Index

Picture Acknowlegements

The publishers would like to thank Carve magazine for supplying all photos in this title: Pete Frieden 4, 16, 29 (bottom, lower middle); Chris van Lennep 10, 29 (upper middle); Tim McKenna 12 (top), 28 (bottom); Chris Power 18 (top), 19 (top), 29 (top); Mike Searle imprint, 5, 6, 7, 8, 11 (both), 12 (bottom), 13 (all pics), 14, 15 (all pics), 17, 18 (bottom), 19, 20, 21 (both), 22 (both), 24 (both), 26 (both), 27, 28 (top, lower middle); Alex Williams (28 upper middle); Darrell Wong 23.

The artwork on pages 8 and 9 was supplied by Mayer Media.